Steve Jobs:
Visionary of the Digital Age

Steven Paul Jobs was born on February 24, 1955, in San Francisco, California, to Joanne Schieble and Abdulfattah Jandali. Adopted by Paul and Clara Jobs shortly after birth, Steve was raised in Mountain View, California, in the heart of what would later become Silicon Valley. Paul Jobs, a machinist, taught Steve how to work with his hands and instilled in him a love for mechanics. Clara Jobs, an accountant, nurtured Steve's interest in education and reading.

From a young age, Steve showed a keen interest in electronics. At the age of 13, he boldly called Bill Hewlett, co-founder of Hewlett-Packard, to ask if he had any spare parts for a frequency counter he was building. Impressed by the young boy's initiative, Hewlett not only provided the parts but also offered Jobs a summer internship at HP. This experience further fueled Jobs' passion for technology and innovation.

Steve was a curious and intelligent child but often found traditional schooling uninspiring. He attended Homestead High School in Cupertino, where he met future Apple co-founder Steve Wozniak through a mutual friend. Despite his lack of enthusiasm for formal education, Jobs showed a keen interest in electronics and gadgetry. After high school, Jobs enrolled at Reed College in Portland, Oregon, but dropped out after one semester. He continued to audit classes, particularly in calligraphy, which would later influence the design aesthetics of Apple products.

Early Career and the Birth of Apple

In 1974, Jobs returned to California and joined Atari, Inc. as a technician. He saved money and later traveled to India in search of spiritual enlightenment, a journey that profoundly impacted his approach to life and business. During this period, Jobs also experimented with LSD, an experience he later described as one of the most important of his life. It helped him gain a different perspective and see the world in new ways. At the same time, his interest in Zen Buddhism began to grow, influenced by his travels and readings. The principles of Zen—mindfulness, simplicity, and focus—became integral to his personal philosophy and shaped his approach to product design and business. Upon returning to the U.S., Jobs reconnected with Wozniak, who was then working on a personal computer design.

In 1976, Jobs and Wozniak founded Apple Computer, Inc. in Jobs' parents' garage. Their first product, the Apple I, was a success among hobbyists and early computer enthusiasts. The following year, they introduced the Apple II, which became one of the first highly successful mass-produced personal computers. The Apple II's success was driven by its user-friendly interface and the ability to display color graphics, a significant innovation at the time.

Revolutionary Products and Leadership Challenges

As Apple grew, Jobs' vision for the company expanded. He recruited experienced executives to help manage the business, including John Sculley, the former president of PepsiCo, whom Jobs famously convinced to join Apple by asking, "Do you want to sell sugar water for the rest of your life, or do you want to come with me and change the world?" Jobs then began focusing on developing new products. In 1984, Apple launched the Macintosh, a revolutionary computer with a graphical user interface that made computing more accessible to the general public. The Macintosh was a significant technological leap, featuring a mouse and a user-friendly interface that set it apart from other computers of the time.

Despite its initial success and the groundbreaking "1984" Super Bowl commercial that announced its arrival, the Macintosh struggled with sales due to its high price and limited software availability. These challenges led to mounting tension between Jobs and Sculley. Jobs wanted to continue pushing the Macintosh aggressively, while Sculley advocated for a more measured approach, focusing on the more profitable Apple II line.

The power struggle between Jobs and Sculley came to a head in 1985 when the board of directors, concerned about Apple losing ground to IBM's PCs, sided with Sculley. This led to Jobs being stripped of his managerial duties. Feeling marginalized and unable to influence the company's direction, Jobs resigned from Apple later that year.

NeXT and Pixar

After leaving Apple, Jobs founded NeXT Inc. in 1985, a computer platform development company focused on the higher-education and business markets. NeXT computers were known for their advanced hardware and software technologies, including an innovative object-oriented software development environment. Despite their technological superiority, NeXT computers were commercially unsuccessful due to their high price and limited market. However, the NeXTSTEP operating system and development environment were highly influential, eventually forming the foundation for Apple's macOS and iOS.

In 1986, Jobs purchased The Graphics Group, which was later renamed Pixar Animation Studios, from Lucasfilm for $10 million. Under his leadership, Pixar transitioned from a struggling graphics company into a groundbreaking animation studio. Pixar's partnership with Disney led to the production of "Toy Story" in 1995, the first feature-length film created entirely with computer-generated imagery (CGI). "Toy Story" was a massive success, both critically and commercially, and established Pixar as a leader in the animation industry. Jobs' vision and business acumen helped Pixar produce a string of successful films, including "A Bug's Life," "Toy Story 2," and "Monsters, Inc.," which eventually led to Pixar's acquisition by Disney in 2006 for $7.4 billion in stock, making Jobs Disney's largest individual shareholder.

Return to Apple and the Rise to Icon Status

In 1996, Apple acquired NeXT for approximately $429 million, bringing Steve Jobs back to the company he co-founded. His return in 1997 marked the beginning of a transformative era for Apple. Faced with a struggling company and an uncertain future, Jobs quickly set about implementing bold changes aimed at revitalizing Apple.

One of his major strategies was to simplify Apple's bloated product line, focusing on quality over quantity. This approach was exemplified by the launch of the iMac in 1998, a colorful, all-in-one computer that broke away from the drab, boxy designs of the time. The iMac's innovative design and user-friendly interface were not only a commercial success but also played a crucial role in restoring Apple's financial health. This success demonstrated Jobs' ability to blend form and function, clarifying Apple's market strategy and paving the way for future innovation.

Following the iMac's success, Jobs continued to push the boundaries of technology and design. In 2001, Apple introduced the iPod, a portable digital music player that transformed how people listened to music. The iPod's sleek design, ease of use, and impressive storage capacity made it a cultural icon. It was complemented by the launch of the iTunes Store in 2003, which provided a legal and user-friendly platform for purchasing and organizing digital music. This combination revolutionized the music industry, shifting the focus from physical media to digital downloads and paving the way for the future of digital media.

The iPhone and the Era of Smartphones

In 2007, Apple unveiled the iPhone, a revolutionary device that combined a phone, an iPod, and an internet communicator into a single, sleek unit. The iPhone's introduction marked a significant shift in the mobile phone industry. Its intuitive touch interface, which eliminated the need for physical keyboards, allowed users to interact with their devices in a more natural and engaging way. The iPhone's design, featuring a large, high-resolution screen that extended nearly to the edges of the device, set a new standard for mobile aesthetics and usability.

The iPhone's powerful capabilities, including its robust operating system and advanced hardware, quickly made it a commercial success. It initiated the era of smartphones by transforming the way people communicate, access information, and use technology. With its ability to integrate phone calls, music, and internet browsing into one device, the iPhone redefined the concept of a mobile phone.

In 2008, Apple expanded the iPhone's functionality further with the introduction of the App Store. This platform allowed third-party developers to create and distribute applications that users could download directly to their devices. The App Store fostered a vibrant ecosystem of apps, ranging from games and social media to productivity tools and specialized services. This not only enhanced the iPhone's utility but also established it as a versatile, indispensable device. The proliferation of apps transformed how people interact with technology, turning the iPhone into a powerful platform for personal and professional use.

In 2010, Steve Jobs introduced the iPad, a tablet computer designed to fill the gap between smartphones and laptops. The iPad featured a large, high-resolution touchscreen that provided a new way to interact with digital content. Its user-friendly interface and portability made it an attractive option for a wide range of applications, from media consumption to business tasks.

Design Philosophy and Jonathan Ive

Steve Jobs' design philosophy was grounded in simplicity, elegance, and functionality. He aimed to integrate hardware, software, and services to create seamless user experiences, embodying the principle that "less is more" through clean lines, minimalistic interfaces, and intuitive usability.

Jonathan Ive, who joined Apple in 1992 and later became Chief Design Officer, played a crucial role in realizing this vision. His work on iconic products such as the iMac, iPhone, and iPad not only reflected Jobs' design principles but also set new standards in industrial design. Ive's sleek, minimalist designs and meticulous attention to detail were integral to Apple's product aesthetics, with numerous patents highlighting his contributions. The deep professional relationship between Jobs and Ive, characterized by mutual respect and a shared vision, was fundamental in creating products that defined Apple's brand and revolutionized technology and design.

Battle with Illness and Final Years

In 2003, Steve Jobs was diagnosed with a rare and aggressive form of pancreatic cancer known as pancreatic neuroendocrine tumor. Initially, Jobs opted for alternative therapies, such as special diets and holistic treatments, and delayed conventional medical interventions like surgery and chemotherapy. This choice was controversial and raised concerns among his family and medical professionals. Despite his illness, Jobs remained deeply engaged in his work, overseeing the development of groundbreaking products and guiding Apple through a period of remarkable growth.

As his health declined in August 2011, Jobs resigned as CEO of Apple, passing the leadership to Tim Cook, who had been groomed as his successor. Jobs continued to serve as Chairman of the Board, providing strategic direction until his health prevented him from fulfilling this role. Steve Jobs passed away on October 5, 2011, at the age of 56. His death elicited a global outpouring of grief and admiration, underscoring the profound impact he had on technology, business, and popular culture. Tributes from around the world celebrated his visionary achievements and the enduring influence he left across various industries.

Leadership Style, Legacy, and Enduring Impact

Known for his demanding and sometimes abrasive management style, Steve Jobs had a keen eye for detail and an unrelenting drive for perfection. Although his approach could be polarizing, it inspired teams to achieve extraordinary results. A master storyteller, Jobs captivated audiences with his theatrical and clear product launch presentations, showcasing his visionary ideas.

Jobs' commitment to integrating design principles into every aspect of Apple's operations, including marketing and branding, shaped the company's distinct identity. He believed that good design should be evident in how the company presented itself and communicated with its audience, setting new benchmarks for excellence in the tech industry.

His 2005 commencement speech at Stanford University epitomized his personal philosophy. In this acclaimed address, Jobs shared profound insights on life, failure, and the pursuit of passion, speaking candidly about his own journey and battle with cancer. He emphasized following one's heart and intuition, even amidst adversity. The speech resonated deeply, reflecting his belief in living authentically and embracing life's uncertainties.

Steve Jobs left a legacy of innovation and creativity that continues to influence the tech industry. Under his leadership, Apple became one of the most valuable and influential companies globally. Jobs' vision of integrating technology seamlessly into everyday life has become a reality, with Apple products now ubiquitous in homes, workplaces, and schools. His contributions—from the Macintosh to the iPhone—have reshaped how people live, work, and play, securing his place as one of the most influential figures in modern history.

—

Next, we explore Steve Jobs' insights and wisdom through a collection of quotes that highlight his innovative spirit and visionary thinking. These reflections offer a glimpse into his views on technology, leadership, and creativity. Enjoy the words of a man who transformed industries and inspired many with his bold approach to life and work.

For the past 33 years,
I have looked in the
mirror every morning
and asked myself:
'If today were the last
day of my life, would
I want to do what I am
about to do today?'
And whenever the
answer has been 'No'
for too many days in
a row, I know I need
to change something.

Creativity is just connecting things. When you ask creative people how they did something, they feel a little guilty because they didn't really do it, they just saw something. It seemed obvious to them after a while. That's because they were able to connect experiences they've had and synthesize new things.

I don't think of
my life as a career.
I do stuff. I respond
to stuff. That's not a
career - it's a life!

When a good idea comes,
part of my job is to
move it around, just
see what different
people think, get
people talking about
it, argue with people
about it, get ideas
moving among that
group of 100 people,
get different people
together to explore
different aspects of it
quietly, and, you know
- just explore things.

When you're a
carpenter crafting a
beautiful chest of
drawers, you wouldn't
use plywood for the
back, even though it
faces the wall and
won't be seen. The
knowledge that it's
there drives you to
use quality wood. For
you to sleep well at
night, the aesthetic,
the quality, has to be
carried all the way
through.

The heaviness of
being successful
was replaced by the
lightness of being
a beginner again,
less sure about
everything. It freed
me to enter one of the
most creative periods
of my life.

(Steve Jobs reflecting on the time
he was fired from Apple)

It's technology
married with liberal
arts, married with
the humanities, that
yields us the results
that make our heart
sing.

You can't connect the dots looking forward; you can only connect them looking backwards. So you have to trust that the dots will somehow connect in your future. You have to trust in something - your gut, destiny, life, karma, whatever. This approach has never let me down, and it has made all the difference in my life.

Here's to the crazy ones,
the misfits, the rebels,
the troublemakers, the
round pegs in the square
holes... the ones who see
things differently -
they're not fond of
rules... You can quote
them, disagree with
them, glorify or vilify
them, but the only thing
you can't do is ignore
them because they
change things.

Good PR educates
people; that's all
it is. You can't
con people in
this business.
The products
speak for
themselves.

It's rare that you
see an artist in his
30s or 40s able to
really contribute
something amazing.
Of course, there are
some people who are
innately curious,
forever little kids
in their awe of life,
but they're rare.

It wasn't all romantic.
I didn't have a dorm
room, so I slept on the
floor in friends' rooms,
I returned coke bottles
for the 5¢ deposits to
buy food with, and I
would walk the 7 miles
across town every
Sunday night to get one
good meal a week at the
Hare Krishna temple.
I loved it.

(Reflecting on his time during
which he dropped out of college)

People think focus means saying yes to the thing you've got to focus on. But that's not what it means at all. It means saying no to the hundred other good ideas that there are. You have to pick carefully. I'm actually as proud of the things we haven't done as the things I have done. Innovation is saying no to a thousand things.

My model for business is
The Beatles. They were
four guys who kept each
other kind of negative
tendencies in check.
They balanced each
other and the total was
greater than the sum of
the parts. That's how I
see business: great
things in business are
never done by one
person, they're done
by a team of people.

At 75, Polaroid's Dr. Edwin Land dedicated the rest of his life to pure scientific research, trying to crack the code of color vision. He's truly a national treasure. I can't fathom why individuals like him aren't celebrated as role models. This is the pinnacle of achievement, more so than being an astronaut or a football player.

I wish him the best,
I really do. I just
think he and
Microsoft are a
bit narrow. He'd be a
broader guy if he had
dropped acid once or
gone off to an ashram
when he was younger.

(On Bill Gates as quoted in
"Creating Jobs" in The New York
Times (12 January 1997))

I would trade all
of my technology
for an afternoon
with Socrates.

As individuals, people are inherently good. I have a somewhat more pessimistic view of people in groups. And I remain extremely concerned when I see what's happening in our country, which is in many ways the luckiest place in the world. We don't seem to be excited about making our country a better place for our kids.

Remembering that I'll be dead soon is the most important tool I've ever encountered to help me make the big choices in life. Because almost everything - all external expectations, all pride, all fear of embarrassment or failure - these things just fall away in the face of death, leaving only what is truly important.

We're gambling on
our vision, and we
would rather do that
than make "me too"
products. Let some
other companies do
that. For us, it's
always the next
dream.

I was at Reed [College]
for only a few months.
My parents intended
for me to stay there
for all four years
but I decided that
college wasn't right
for me. I had no idea
what I wanted to do I
didn't see how college
was going to help me.

Your time is
limited, so don't
waste it living
someone else's life.
Don't be trapped by
dogma - which is
living with the
results of other
people's thinking.
Don't let the noise
of others' opinions
drown out your own
inner voice.

Taking LSD had a profound impact on me, ranking among the most crucial experiences of my life. It showed me an alternate view of reality, which you can't remember once it wears off, but you know it exists. It reinforced my sense of what was important—creating great things instead of making money, putting things back into the stream of history and of human consciousness as much as I could.

Most PC companies have lost their engineering expertise. Consumer electronics companies don't grasp the software aspects. As a result, the products Apple creates can't be replicated elsewhere. Apple's the only company that has everything under one roof.

The mark of an
innovative company
is not only that it
comes up with new
ideas first, but also
that it knows how to
leapfrog when it
finds itself behind.

There's an old Wayne
Gretzky quote that I
love. 'I skate to where
the puck is going to
be, not where it has
been.' And we've
always tried to do
that at Apple. Since
the very, very
beginning. And
we always will.

If you want to live
your life in a
creative way, as an
artist, you have to
not look back too
much. You have to be
willing to take
whatever you've done
and whoever you were
and throw them away.

I think if you do
something and it
turns out pretty
good, then you
should go do
something else
wonderful, not
dwell on it for too
long. Just figure
out what's next.

It takes a lot of
hard work to make
something simple,
to truly understand
the underlying
challenges and come
up with elegant
solutions.

You can tell a lot
about a person by
who his or her
heroes are.

Innovation requires continuous effort. Dylan could have stuck to singing protest songs and likely made a lot of money, but he chose to evolve. When he went electric in 1965, he alienated many fans, but his 1966 European tour became legendary. Similarly, The Beatles constantly evolved, refining their music. This is what I strive for — continuous progress. As Dylan puts it, if you're not busy being born, you're busy dying.

You've got to find what you love. And that is as true for your work as it is for your lovers. Your work is going to fill a large part of your life, and the only way to be truly satisfied is to do what you believe is great work. And the only way to do great work is to love what you do.

My passion has been to build an enduring company where people were motivated to make great products; the products, not the profits, were the motivation. Sculley flipped these priorities to where the goal was to make money. It's a subtle difference, but it ends up meaning everything.

CONTEXT: Steve Jobs hired John Sculley from PepsiCo in 1983, but their differing priorities—Jobs focusing on product innovation and Sculley on profitability—led to conflicts and ultimately Jobs' departure from Apple in 1985.

No one wants to
die. Even people
who want to go to
heaven don't want
to die to get there.

Everything around you
that you call life was
made up by people that
were no smarter than
you and you can change
it, you can influence
it, you can build your
own things that other
people can use. Once
you learn that, you'll
never be the same
again.

I always thought of myself as a humanities person as a kid, but I liked electronics. Then I read something that one of my heroes, Edwin Land of Polaroid, said about the importance of people who could stand at the intersection of humanities and sciences, and I decided that's what I wanted to do.

I can help the next
generation remember
the lineage of great
companies here and
how to continue
the tradition.
The Valley has been
very supportive of
me. I should do my
best to repay.

Simplicity is not
just minimalism
or the absence of
clutter. It involves
digging through the
depth of complexity.
To be truly simple,
you have to go
really deep.

Intuition is a very
powerful thing,
more powerful
than intellect.

We hired truly great
people and gave them
the room to do great
work. A lot of
companies [...] hire
people to tell them
what to do. We hire
people to tell us what
to do. We figure we're
paying them all this
money; their job is to
figure out what to do
and tell us.

When you grow up, you tend to get told that the world is the way it is, and your life is just to live your life inside the world. Try not to bash into the walls too much. Try to have a nice family life. Have fun, save a little money. That's a very limited life. Life can be much broader.

Have the courage to
follow your heart
and intuition.
They somehow
already know what
you truly want to
become. Everything
else is secondary.

I hate it when people
call themselves
'entrepreneurs' when
what they're really
trying to do is launch a
startup and then sell of
go public, so they can
cash in and move on.
They're unwilling to do
the work it takes to
build a real company,
which is the hardest
work in business.

Sometimes when
you innovate, you
make mistakes. It
is best to admit
them quickly,
and get on with
improving your
other innovations.

We built Mac for
ourselves. We were the
group of people who
were going to judge
whether it was great or
not. We weren't going to
go out and do market
research. We just
wanted to build the
best thing we could
build.

(In a 1985 interview with Playboy,
following the debut of the
Macintosh)

Most people never pick up
the phone and call. Most
people never ask, and
that's what separates the
people who do things from
the people who just dream
about them. You have to act,
and you have to be willing
to fail. You have to be
willing to crash and burn,
because if you are afraid
of failing, you will not
get very far.

(recalling the time he called up Bill
Hewlett of Hewlett-Packard as a kid
for parts for his electronics project)

Apple has some
tremendous assets,
but I believe without
some attention, the
company could, could,
could — I'm searching
for the right word —
could, could die.

(On his return as interim CEO of
Apple, as quoted in TIME magazine
(18 August 1997))

You have to deeply
understand the
essence of a product
in order to be able
to get rid of the
parts that are not
essential.

You've got to have an idea, or a problem or a wrong that you want to right that you're passionate about otherwise you're not going to have the perseverance to stick it through. I think that's half the battle right there.

What a computer is to
me is it's the most
remarkable tool that we
have ever come up with.
It's the equivalent of a
bicycle for our minds.

(Speaking in the documentary
Memory and Imagination:
New Pathways to the Library
of Congress (1991))

We have always
been shameless
about stealing
great ideas.

If you haven't found
it yet, keep looking.
Don't settle. As with
all matters of the
heart, you'll know
when you find it.
And, like any great
relationship, it just
gets better and
better as the years
roll on. So keep
looking. Don't
settle.

Nobody has tried to swallow us since I've been here. I think they are afraid how we would taste.

(At the annual Apple shareholder meeting (22 April, 1998))

We're going to be able
to ask our computers
to monitor things for
us, and when certain
conditions happen,
are triggered, the
computers will take
certain actions and
inform us after the
fact.

I had been
rejected, but I was
still in love. And
so I decided to
start over.

(Reflecting on the time
he was fired from Apple)

People get stuck as they get older... Your thoughts construct patterns like scaffolding in your mind. You are really etching chemical patterns. In most cases, people get stuck in those patterns, just like grooves in a record, and they never get out of them.

Pixar is the most
technically advanced
creative company;
Apple is the most
creatively advanced
technical company.

(Fortune magazine,
February 21, 2005)

I'm the only person I know that's lost a quarter of a billion dollars in one year.... It's very character-building.

(As quoted in Apple Confidential 2.0: The Definitive History of the World's Most Colorful Company by Owen W. Linzmayer, 2004)

The reason that Apple is
able to create products
like iPad is because we
always try to be at the
intersection of
technology and liberal
arts, to be able to get
the best of both.

I feel like somebody just
punched me in the stomach
and knocked all my wind
out. I'm only 30 years old
and I want to have a
chance to continue
creating things. I know
I've got at least one more
great computer in me. And
Apple is not going to give
me a chance to do that.

(On his expulsion from any position
of authority at Apple, after having
invited John Sculley to become CEO,
as quoted in Playboy (September 1987))

Every once in a while a
revolutionary product
comes along that
changes everything.
It's very fortunate if
you can work on just
one of these in your
career. ... Apple's been
very fortunate in that
it's introduced a few
of these.

At first glance, a problem might seem simple because you don't yet see its full complexity. As you dig deeper, you discover it's actually quite complicated and come up with complex solutions. This is where most people give up. However, a truly great person will persist until they uncover the underlying principle of the problem and develop a simple, elegant solution that works.

Sometimes life hits
you in the head with
a brick. Don't lose
faith. I'm convinced
that the only thing
that kept me going
was that I loved
what I did.

That's been one of my
mantras – focus and
simplicity. Simple
can be harder than
complex: You have to
work hard to get your
thinking clean to
make it simple. But
it's worth it in the
end because once you
get there, you can
move mountains.

You'll see more and more perfection of that - computer as servant. But the next thing is going to be computer as a guide or agent.

My mother taught me to read before I went to school, so I was pretty bored in school, and I turned into a little terror. You should have seen us in third grade. We basically destroyed our teacher. We would let snakes loose in the classroom and explode bombs.

For something
this complicated,
it's really hard to
design products by
focus groups. A lot
of times, people
don't know what
they want until
you show it to
them.

Recruiting is challenging; it's like finding needles in a haystack. A one-hour interview isn't enough to uncover everything. Ultimately, it comes down to your gut feeling. How do you perceive this candidate? How do they respond to challenges? I ask everyone, 'Why are you here?' The specific answers are less important than the meta-data they reveal.

When you're young,
you might think that
television networks are
conspiring to dumb us
down. But as you get older,
you realize that's not the
case. The networks simply
provide what people want.
This realization is even
more disheartening than a
conspiracy because it
means there's no one to
overthrow; the networks
are just catering to public
demand. It's a sobering
truth.

As companies scale into billion-dollar giants, they often lose their initial vision. They introduce numerous levels of middle management, which creates a disconnect between the leaders and the workers. This results in a loss of genuine passion for the products. The creative minds, who are truly invested, must persuade multiple managerial layers to achieve what they believe is right.

The problem with
the Internet startup
craze isn't that too
many people are
starting companies;
it's that too many
people aren't
sticking with it.

First was the mouse.
The second was the
click wheel. And now,
we're going to bring
multi-touch to the
market. And each of
these revolutionary
interfaces has
made possible a
revolutionary product
– the Mac, the iPod and
now the iPhone.

(speaking at the iPhone 2007
Presentation)

A lot of people in
our industry haven't
had very diverse
experiences. So they
don't have enough dots
to connect, and they end
up with very linear
solutions without a
broad perspective on
the problem. The broader
one's understanding of
the human experience,
the better design we
will have.

Someone once told me, 'Manage the top line, and the bottom line will follow.' So, what is the top line? It's questions like, why are we doing this? What's our strategy? What feedback are we getting from customers? How responsive are we? Do we have the best products and people? These are the essential questions to focus on.

You've got to start
with the customer
experience and
work back toward
the technology -
not the other way
around.

The axis today is
not liberal and
conservative,
the axis is
constructive-
destructive.

Everybody in this
country should
learn how to
program a computer,
because it teaches
you how to think.

When I hire someone for a high-level role, their competence is a given—they need to be very smart. But what truly matters is whether they will become passionate about Apple. If they do, everything else will follow naturally. They'll be driven to do what's best for Apple, rather than focusing on their own interests or those of others.

People think it's this veneer — that the designers are handed this box and told, 'Make it look good!' That's not what we think design is. It's not just what it looks like and feels like. Design is how it works.

Part of what made
the Macintosh great
was that the people
working on it were
musicians and poets
and artists and
zoologists and
historians who also
happened to be the
best computer
scientists in the
world.

Miele really thought
the process through.
They did such a great
job designing these
washers and dryers.
I got more thrill out
of them than I have
out of any piece of
high tech in years.

(Speaking of the design excellence
of Miele, a high-quality German
appliance brand, in a February
1996 interview with WIRED
magazine)

Creativity comes
from spontaneous
meetings,
from random
discussions.

I'm convinced that
about half of what
separates successful
entrepreneurs from
the non-successful
ones is pure
perseverance.

Everyone here has
the sense that right
now is one of those
moments when we are
influencing the
future.

(Steve Jobs interview with
Playboy magazine – A discussion
with David Sheff, February 1985)

Woz and I started
Apple in my parents'
garage when I was 20.
We worked hard, and
in 10 years Apple had
grown from just the
two of us in a garage
into a $2 billion
company with over
4,000 employees.

My favorite things in
life don't cost any
money. It's really
clear that the most
precious resource
we all have is time.

This revolution,
the information
revolution, is a
revolution of free
energy as well, but
of another kind:
free intellectual
energy.

[They] push the human race forward, and while some may see them as the crazy ones, we see genius, because the ones who are crazy enough to think they can change the world, are the ones who do.

Being the richest
man in the cemetery
doesn't matter to me
... Going to bed at
night saying we've
done something
wonderful... that's
what matters to me.

If Macintosh hadn't
been successful, then
I should have just
thrown in the towel,
because my vision of
the whole industry
would have been
totally wrong.

(Playboy, Feb. 1985)

The bottom line is, I didn't return to Apple for the money. I've been very lucky and already have a substantial fortune. By the time I was 25, I had around $100 million. I made a decision then not to let it dominate my life. There's no way to spend it all, and I don't equate wealth with intelligence.

Remembering that
you are going to die
is the best way I
know to avoid the
trap of thinking you
have something to
lose. You are already
naked. There is no
reason not to follow
your heart.

Stay Hungry. Stay
Foolish. And I have
always wished that
for myself. And now,
as you graduate to
begin anew, I wish
that for you. Stay
Hungry. Stay
Foolish.

No one has ever escaped death. And that is as it should be, because Death is very likely the single best invention of Life. It is Life's change agent. It clears out the old to make way for the new.

Major Lessons from the Life of Steve Jobs

PURSUE PASSION RELENTLESSLY – Steve Jobs' passion for design and technology was the driving force behind his numerous innovations. His intense focus on creating products he genuinely cared about helped him overcome numerous obstacles and push the boundaries of what was possible. This relentless pursuit of passion led to the creation of groundbreaking products like the Macintosh, iPod, iPhone, and iPad. Jobs' story teaches us that following our passions with unwavering dedication can lead to remarkable achievements and inspire others to share in our vision.

DON'T FEAR FAILURE – Steve Jobs faced numerous setbacks throughout his career, including being ousted from the very company he co-founded. However, he viewed these failures as opportunities to learn and grow. After leaving Apple, he founded NeXT and acquired Pixar, both of which achieved significant success. His eventual return to Apple marked a period of unprecedented innovation and growth for the company. Jobs' resilience in the face of failure underscores the importance of perseverance and the ability to view setbacks as valuable lessons rather than insurmountable obstacles.

EMBRACE INNOVATION – Jobs consistently championed innovation by not only improving existing products but also rethinking them from the ground up. He believed that true innovation comes from a deep understanding of both technology and human needs. This mindset led to the development of products that transformed industries and the way we live. For example, the iPhone revolutionized mobile communication, and the iPad redefined personal computing. Jobs' approach encourages us to look beyond incremental improvements and seek revolutionary changes that can redefine our world.

DESIGN MATTERS – Jobs placed high value on aesthetics and user experience, believing that great design was as important as functionality. His commitment to design excellence showed that form and function should go hand in hand. Under his leadership, Apple created products that were not only technologically advanced but also visually appealing and intuitive to use. This focus on design has been a key factor in Apple's success, illustrating the importance of considering user experience in product development. Jobs' philosophy teaches us that attention to design can elevate a product from good to extraordinary.

FOCUS ON QUALITY – Jobs was known for his attention to detail and his insistence on high-quality products. He believed that focusing on quality—even if it meant making tough decisions and taking longer to develop a product—was crucial for long-term success. This commitment to excellence is evident in Apple's products, which are renowned for their reliability, performance, and craftsmanship. Jobs' emphasis on quality teaches us that striving for the highest standards can set a company apart from its competitors and build lasting customer loyalty.

THINK DIFFERENTLY – Steve Jobs' famous slogan, "Think Different," encapsulates his unique approach to problem-solving. Jobs encouraged questioning the status quo and pursuing unconventional paths to achieve extraordinary results. He believed that creativity and innovation stem from thinking outside traditional boundaries and exploring new perspectives. This mindset led to the creation of products that were not only innovative but also transformative. By embracing a "Think Different" philosophy, Jobs challenged his team and the world to look beyond conventional wisdom and seek new and groundbreaking solutions.

LEADERSHIP AND VISION- Jobs' leadership style was both inspiring and demanding. He had a clear and compelling vision for Apple and was able to communicate it effectively to his team. His ability to articulate this vision and his unwavering commitment to it were key to rallying people around him. Jobs was known for pushing his team to achieve the highest standards, often demanding excellence and innovation. His leadership style, while sometimes controversial, fostered a culture of creativity and excellence within Apple. Jobs' example demonstrates the importance of having a strong vision and the ability to inspire others to pursue it with passion and dedication.

PRIORITIZE USER EXPERIENCE – Jobs was obsessed with how products felt and worked in users' hands. He placed a high priority on user experience, ensuring that Apple's products were not only functional but also intuitive and enjoyable to use. This focus led to the development of interfaces that were easy to navigate and seamless integration across Apple's ecosystem. Jobs understood that a product's success depended on how well it resonated with users, and he constantly sought to improve the user experience. His emphasis on prioritizing user experience teaches us that understanding and meeting the needs of users is essential for creating products that people love.

BE DETAIL-ORIENTED – Jobs' meticulous attention to detail extended to every aspect of Apple's products, from hardware to software. He believed that every element of a product, no matter how small, contributed to the overall user experience. This commitment to detail often set Apple's offerings apart from competitors. Jobs' insistence on perfection led to products that were not only beautiful and functional but also reliable and consistent. His focus on the finer details teaches us that excellence is achieved through a relentless pursuit of perfection and an unwavering commitment to quality.

BALANCE BUSINESS AND CREATIVITY – Jobs had a unique ability to combine business acumen with creative vision. He understood that for innovative ideas to succeed, they needed to be backed by a solid business strategy. Jobs was able to navigate the complexities of the business world while fostering a culture of creativity and innovation within Apple. He knew how to balance the financial and operational aspects of running a company with the creative processes necessary for innovation. This ability to integrate business and creativity was crucial to Apple's success and serves as a valuable lesson in how to achieve sustainable growth and innovation in any industry.

--

Reflecting on Steve Jobs' life reveals key lessons about success and innovation. His journey highlights the value of passion, resilience, and vision. If you enjoyed these insights, please visit our author page for more inspiring titles.